04

LIFE CYCLES

Snakes

By Melanie Mitchell

first step nonfiction

Lerner Publications Company · Minneapolis

Look at the **snake**.

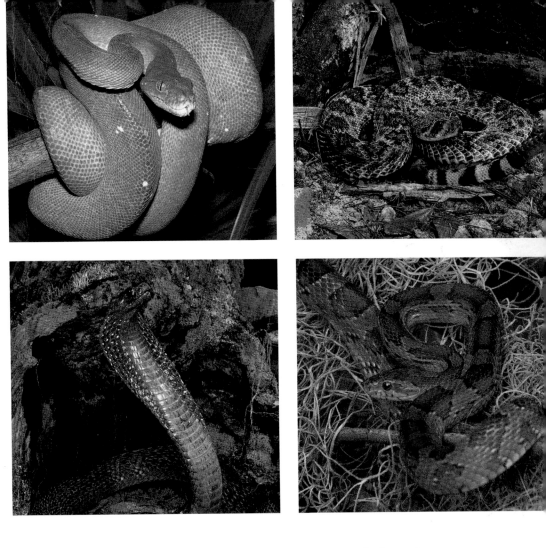

There are many kinds
of snakes.

A snake is a **reptile**, like
a **lizard** or a **turtle**.

4

How does a snake grow?

Some snakes are born as
tiny snakes.

Garter snakes start life
this way.

Some snakes come
from eggs.

Milk snakes come
from eggs.

The baby snakes **hatch**
from eggs.

After they hatch, the baby
snakes leave the nest.

Baby snakes hunt for food.

They eat frogs and mice.

The baby snakes grow
bigger.

They grow out of their skin.

This snake is grown up.

It is fun to watch a
snake grow.

Parts of a Snake

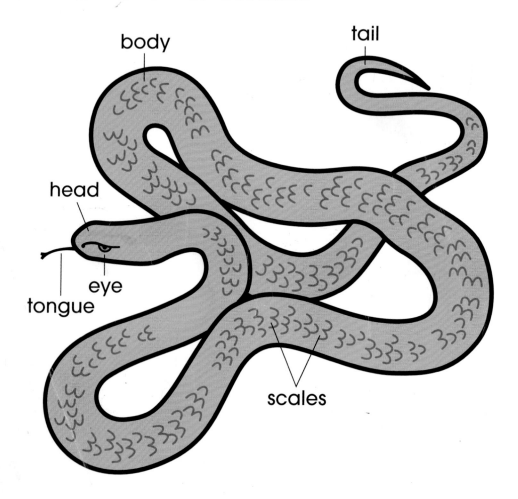

body

tail

head

eye

tongue

scales

Adult Snakes

There are many kinds and sizes of adult snakes. All snakes have the same basic body parts. Snakes have a tongue that is used for smelling, not tasting. A snake's entire body is covered with scales. Snakes slide along the ground using their stomach muscles.

In the winter, most adult snakes hibernate, or sleep. When they wake up they hunt for food. In the spring, they lay eggs or have babies. A new snake life cycle begins.

Snake Fun Facts

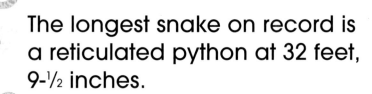

The longest snake on record is a reticulated python at 32 feet, 9-½ inches.

The heaviest snake is an anaconda, weighing about 600 pounds.

Snakes are cold-blooded animals. Their body temperature is the same as the air around them.

Snakes do not have eyelids or ears.

Each time a rattlesnake sheds its skin a new rattle is added to the base of its tail.

A snake's eyes appear cloudy several days before it sheds its skin.

A snake can swallow prey three times bigger than its own mouth. Some large snakes have swallowed whole tigers.

Glossary

 hatch – to come out of an egg

 lizard – a reptile with four legs and a long tail

 reptile – cold-blooded animals that creep or crawl on the ground

 snake – an animal with a long body and no legs

 turtle – an animal with a hard shell covering its body

Index

The photographs in this book are reproduced through the courtesy of: © Allen Blake Sheldon, front cover, pp. 2, 3 (all), 6, 7, 8, 9, 10, 11, 13, 14, 15, 16, 17, 22 (top, middle, second from bottom); © State of Minnesota, Department of Natural Resources, pp. 4, 22 (bottom); © Dan Nedrelo, p. 5; © Michael H. Francis, p. 12; © A.A.M. van der Heyden/Independent Picture Service, p. 22 (second from top).

Illustration on p. 18 by Laura Westlund.

This book is available in two editions:
Library binding by Lerner Publications Company, a division of Lerner Publishing Group
Soft cover by First Avenue Editions, an imprint of Lerner Publishing Group
241 First Avenue North
Minneapolis, MN 55401 U.S.A.

Website address: www.lernerbooks.com

Library of Congress Cataloging-in-Publication Data

Mitchell, Melanie S.
        Snakes / by Melanie S. Mitchell.
            p.   cm. — (First step nonfiction) (Life cycles)
        Summary: A basic overview of the life cycle of a snake
    and the behavior of young snakes as they grow.
        ISBN: 0–8225–4606–X (lib. bdg. : alk. paper)
        ISBN: 0–8225–4607–8 (pbk. : alk. paper)
        1. Snakes—Life cycles—Juvenile literature.
    [1. Snakes. 2. Animals—Infancy.] I. Title. II. Series.
    QL666.O6 M67 2003
    597.96—dc21   2002003279

Manufactured in the United States of America
1 2 3 4 5 6 – JR – 08 07 06 05 04 03